SHAKE, RATTLE AND ROLL

Contents

Written by Maire Buonocore
Illustrated by Nick Duffy and Martin Bedford

Collins Educational

An Imprint of HarperCollinsPublishers

Musical Instruments

Different instruments are played
in different ways. The sounds
instruments produce can be
made by **plucking, blowing,
striking, shaking or stroking.**

These unusual and interesting
instruments come from many
different countries.

Guess how each one is played.

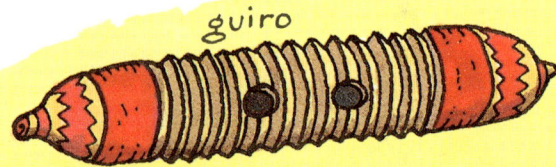

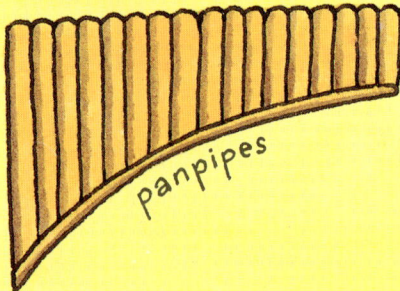

guiro

panpipes

acoustic guitar

maracas

daina

Instruments which are plucked

The earliest instruments to be played by plucking were a kind of bow. The bow was made by tying a length of animal gut to the ends of a strong piece of wood. When the string was plucked it made a musical sound. When the wood was bent it loosened or tightened the string and the note changed. **The sound is made because the string vibrates when it is plucked.**

Some instruments which are played by plucking are…

ukelele

zither

sitar

electric guitar

The strings on these instruments are tuned by turning pegs which tighten or loosen the string and change the pitch of the note.

lute

To make a bow:
Stretch an elastic band around a ruler. Pluck it to hear the note. Stretch the elastic band and pluck it again.

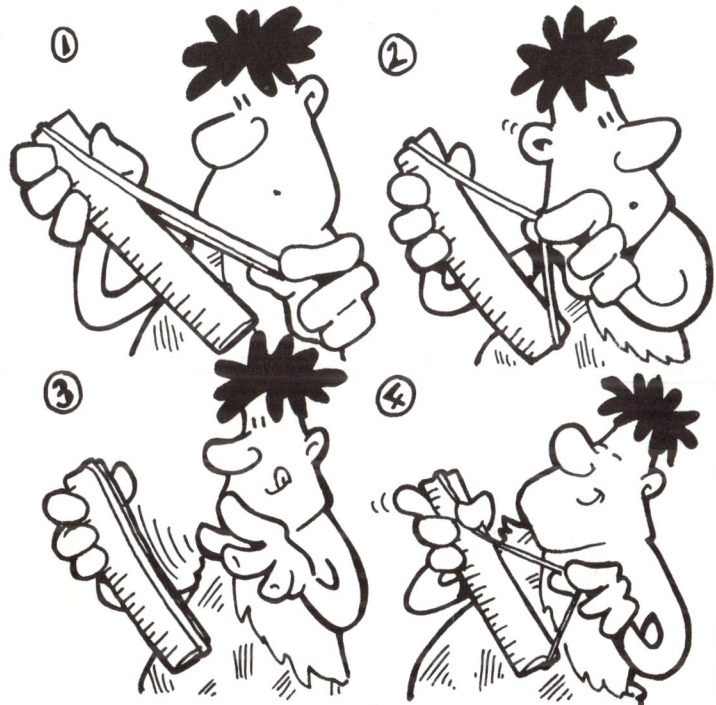

① ② ③ ④

Try to play a tune.

Instruments which are blown

The earliest instruments to be played by blowing were hollow reeds which grew by rivers. The sound was produced by blowing down one end. Reeds of different lengths made different sounds. Animal horns were also blown to make music and were much louder than the reeds. The notes of the horn could be changed by changing the position and shape of the lips. **The sound is made because the air vibrates inside the tube.**

Some instruments which are played by blowing are…

bugle

bagpipes

panpipes

didgeridoo

The notes played on these instruments can be changed by covering and uncovering holes or by blowing harder or more gently.

recorder

Cut 5 jumbo straws to different lengths. Stick them together with tape so that the ends of the straws are level at one edge.

Blow across the level edge to make the sound.

Instruments which are struck

The earliest instruments to be played by striking were a kind of drum. They were made by hollowing out logs and striking them with bones or large sticks. Different parts of the drum made different sounds. Tunes could also be made by hitting stones of different sizes.

The sound is made because the air moves more freely in the middle of the log than at the ends.

Some instruments which are played by striking are...

yunluo

xylophone

steel drum

glockenspiel

Some African drums make many tones. An experienced player can send messages across a village by playing different tones very fast.

ntenga

To make a drum:
Pull clingfilm tightly across the top of an empty tin. Seal it with sticky tape. Tap it with a wooden spoon. Try this again with different size containers.

Listen to the different sounds.

Instruments which are shaken

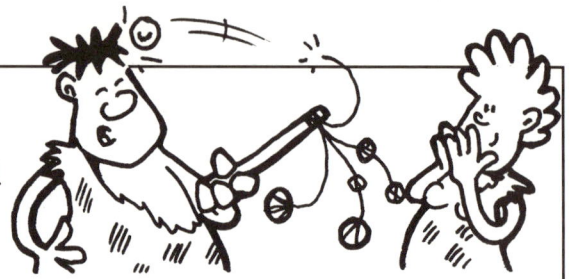

The earliest instruments to be played by shaking were a kind of rattle. Coconut shells were filled with sand or small stones. Stones and shells were threaded onto string or grass and hung on the outside of a calabash (a kind of gourd). Another early shaker was made by tying stones of different sizes onto a stick with string. **Shaking the coconut and calabash shells, makes the sand and stones rattled together.**

Some instruments which are played by **shaking** are…

maracas

cabaca

handbells

Handbells and yunluo (temple bells) are also shaken. They have clappers inside which move backwards and forwards as the bell is shaken.

handbell

To make a shaker:
Scrunch up some metal foil tops and put them into a clear plastic bottle. Put the lid on. Try making shakers with dried peas, small pebbles and sand.

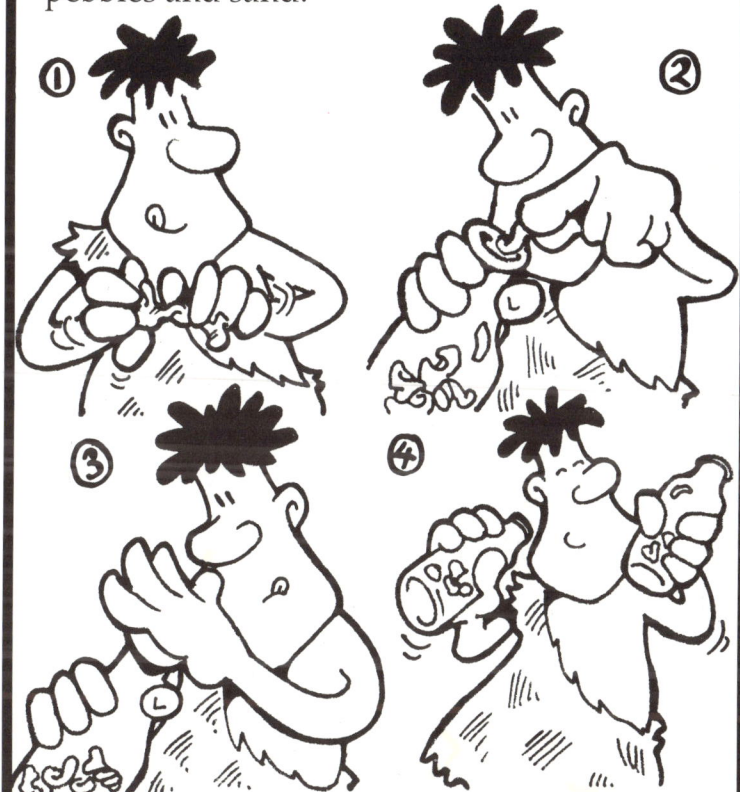

Listen to the different sounds.

Instruments which are stroked

The earliest instruments to be played by stroking were a kind of grater. Notches were made in wooden sticks and another stick was run very quickly up and down along the notches. Later, rasps were made by putting notches on hollowed wood which made the sound much louder. This instrument is still used today. It is called a guiro.

The sound is made by the friction of wood rubbing against wood.

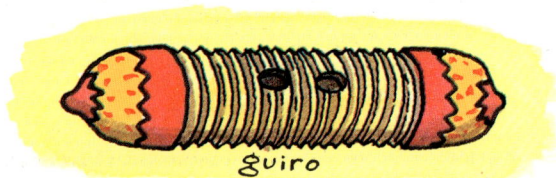

guiro

Instruments in the violin family are played by stroking in a slightly different way. To make a sound from these instruments, a bow is gently stroked across the strings. **The sound is made by making the strings vibrate. The sound is made louder by the sound box.**

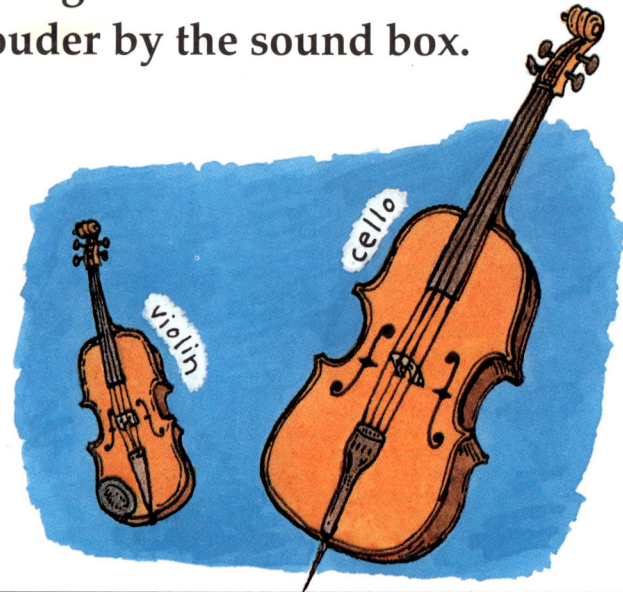

violin

cello

The player can change the note by pressing on the strings. This shortens the length of the string which vibrates and makes the note higher.

violin

To make a glass sing:
Gently stroke the rim of a glass with a wet finger. You will make a sound. Now fill four or five glasses with different amounts of water and repeat the stroking.

Listen to the different tones.

Did you know?

During the **Chinese Dragon** dance at the Chinese New Year celebrations, the more noise there is from the instruments the faster the dragon dances and the higher it leaps.

A **didgeridoo** used to be made from a piece of wood which had been hollowed out by termites. The player has to breathe in through the nose and out through the mouth at the same time (by storing air in the cheeks).

Slaves in galley ships rowed to the rhythm of a drum being beaten. They had to pull the oars every time the drum was hit. The faster the drum was hit, the faster they rowed.

Alpine horns (Alphorns) are made from wood. Swiss herders send messages to each other across mountains using these very long horns.

Cowbells all have different notes. A farmer can remember the sound of each cow's bell and can hear if the cow has wandered away from the meadow.

Index